HOW TO STOP BEFORE YOU POP

An Anger-Management Program For Grades 3-5

By Kathie Guild

HOW TO STOP BEFORE YOU POP

10-DIGIT ISBN: 1-57543-146-7   13-DIGIT ISBN: 978-1-57543-146-8

GRAPHIC DESIGN/LAYOUT: Cameon Funk

COPYRIGHT © 2007 MAR*CO PRODUCTS, INC.
Published by mar*co products, inc.
1443 Old York Road
Warminster, PA 18974
1-800-448-2197
www.marcoproducts.com

PRINTED IN THE U.S.A.

Table Of Contents

How To Stop Before You

The *How To Stop Before You Pop* curriculum consists of various activities, science experiments, role-plays, class discussions, and student activity sheets focused on helping students identify and deal with sources of conflict while teaching communication skills and anger-management strategies. The curriculum is divided into six lessons best presented in sequential order. The lessons include enough material to cover 12 conflict-management classes. The curriculum is intended for Grades 3-5. Each lesson is approximately 45 minutes long.

Lesson 1: *Conflict* is defined, and students are asked to identify sources of conflict in their personal lives. Physical reactions to conflict are described, and students rate their individual levels of tolerance for managing conflict.

Lesson 2: The students focus on calming strategies. Basic stress-reduction skills are introduced and practiced, and the students are asked to identify visual imagery they can use to help calm themselves down. They are then given an experiment to raise their tolerance for frustration and asked to use a calming strategy in order to complete the task.

Lesson 3: This lesson teaches students about the personal power each of them has and the connection between their thoughts and their feelings. The students are taught ways to manage their negative thoughts in order to more effectively control their feelings.

The fourth and fifth lessons are aimed at both verbal and nonverbal communication. These lessons teach the students the ways that good communication skills can be instrumental in resolving conflicts.

Lesson 4: This lesson illustrates the importance of nonverbal communication. The students learn how to recognize their own body language and effectively read the body language of others.

Lesson 5: "I" Messages are introduced as a way to communicate effectively. Each student is paired with another student, assigned a problem situation, and asked to construct an "I" Message. Each pair then role-plays the problem and the "I" Message solution they devised.

Lesson 6: The curriculum is reviewed. Then students are assigned to groups and asked to apply the skills learned in previous lessons. Depending on the students' ages and abilities, the concluding activities on the activity sheets may be completed independently or with guidance from the counselor or teacher.

A *Pre/Post Test* (page 6) is included for those who wish to evaluate the program.

How To Stop Before You Pop

NAME _____ DATE_____

Directions: Read each statement. If you know the answer, circle **T** for **True** or **F** for **False**. If you do not know the answer, circle **DK** for **Don't Know**.

1. Anger is a bad emotion that should never be expressed or shown.

   T   F   DK

2. No good has ever come from conflict or from being angry.

   T   F   DK

3. The two main reasons for conflict between people are differences between values/needs and possessions/resources.

   T   F   DK

4. We have physical reactions when we are involved in a conflict or are mad.

   T   F   DK

5. When you are mad, you should not slow down and try to regain your balance. Speed up and do the first thing that pops into your head.

   T   F   DK

6. When you feel like you have a tornado inside your body, you feel calm.

   T   F   DK

7. Your thoughts control your feelings.

   T   F   DK

8. A *Power Test* shows how much weight you can lift.

   T   F   DK

9. Body language or nonverbal communication can be hidden and hard to read.

   T   F   DK

10. "I" Messages are a way to communicate your feelings.

    T   F   DK

How To Stop Before You Pop

1. **False.** Anger is a natural human reaction and is not bad. The key is to learn how to express anger in a positive way.

2. **False.** Anger or conflict can be positive when channeled in the right direction. Many positive movements have resulted from anger or conflict. Examples of these movements are civil rights activism, the fight to obtain women's suffrage, and Mothers Against Drunk Driving (MADD).

3. **True.** Most of our conflict is rooted in values/needs or possessions/resources.

4. **True.** Anger produces physical reactions in all of us. Learning to recognize these reactions is a critical element of conflict resolution.

5. **False.** When you are really angry, it is best to try to slow things down. Slowing the pace allows you to harness your emotions while giving your brain an opportunity to solve the problem rationally.

6. **False.** *Tornado feelings* often signify a lack of control. Tornado feelings are the opposite of calm feelings.

7. **True.** What we *think* is what we *feel.* Our thoughts dictate our feelings. When we control our thoughts, we control our feelings.

8. **False.** A *Power Test* is not about bench-pressing. *Power Tests* involve having power over your own thoughts and, therefore, power over your feelings.

9. **True.** Nonverbal communication or body language may be hard to interpret and is often misunderstood.

10. **True.** "I" Messages are an effective and positive way to express your feelings.

Lesson Plans

How To Stop Before You Pop

Materials Needed:

For the leader:
- ☐ Bubble wrap (large bubbles)
- ☐ Chalkboard and chalk or white board and markers
- ☐ Glass bottle with a cork
- ☐ Vinegar
- ☐ Baking soda
- ☐ Glass bottle with screw-on cap
- ☐ Oil
- ☐ Water
- ☐ Blue food coloring
- ☐ 3 tennis balls, preferably of different colors
- ☐ Scissors or sharp knife
- ☐ Transparency of *Anger Mountain* (optional, page 23)
- ☐ Overhead projector (optional)

For each student:
- ☐ Copy of *What Groups Do I Belong To?* (page 20)
- ☐ Copy of *My Rate Of Popping* (page 21)
- ☐ Copy of *My Physical Signs* (page 22)
- ☐ Copy of *What Are My Poppers?* (page 24)
- ☐ Pencil

Optional items for purchase:
- ☐ Poppers: Oriental Trading Company, 5455 S. 90th Street, Omaha, Nebraska 68127. 1-800-875-8480. www.orientaltrading.com
- ☐ Bubble Wrap: Staples. 1-800-3STAPLE. www.staples.com

Lesson:

Introduce the lesson by saying:

For the next few weeks, I will be coming in to talk with you about different ways to handle conflict. I hope to teach you specific strategies and skills that will calm you down when you get really angry and will help you resolve the conflict.

There is nothing wrong with feeling angry. Anger is a normal, healthy emotion that everyone feels and should express. People sometimes think the way to resolve conflict is to swallow their anger or not show that they are mad. That is not true. It is OK to let others know you are angry or upset, but you must show your emotion in a way that does not involve hurting someone or breaking something.

Show the students the bubble wrap. Then say:

Many of you have seen bubble wrap before. We use it to wrap fragile things so they won't break. I brought it along because it is a good way to demonstrate what anger sounds like when it is released. The bubble wrap expresses itself, but does not do any damage. That is what you will be learning to do with your anger.

Raise your hand if you ever get mad. (Pop one bubble on the bubble wrap.) *Raise both hands if you ever get really mad.* (Pop two bubbles on the bubble wrap.) *Wiggle your fingers if you ever get really, really mad.* (Pop three bubbles on the bubble wrap.) *Wave your arms if you ever get so mad that you feel like you are going to explode, pop, or lose control.* (Pop several bubbles on the bubble wrap.)

All of us have different popping levels and different things that make us pop. In order for us to gain control over our emotions and over the sources of our conflict, it is important for us to know what things make us pop and how much we can stand before we do pop.

I have been using the word conflict *quite a bit. What does the word* conflict *mean?* (Pause for responses.) **Conflict** *occurs when you disagree with a person or a group of people about how a situation should be resolved. A large conflict involves countries rather than individuals and is referred to as a* **war.** *Most conflicts involve possessions and resources or values and needs.*

On the board, write:

THE TWO MAIN SOURCES OF CONFLICT

    1. Possessions/Resources
    2. Values/Needs

Then continue the lesson by saying:

The first source of conflict is possessions *and* resources. *Conflicts over possessions and resources occur when you want something that someone else has. This might be land, a house, shoes, clothes, a CD, etc. Some relationship problems fall into this category. If your best friend starts hanging out with someone else, for example, you may get possessive and blame the new friend. You might think this new person is "stealing" your old friend away from you. Another common problem in this conflict category is* copying. *If someone else starts using an expression you use a lot or dressing like you do, this could be the source of a conflict over possessions and resources.*

The second source of conflict concerns **values and needs. This type of conflict occurs when people have very different viewpoints on an important topic or way of thinking. An example of this type of conflict would be between animal rights activists and people who make fur coats. Animal rights activists believe that animals should not be killed to make clothing. Furriers believe it is OK to use animals in this way as long as they are killed humanely.**

Differences of opinion about gun control fall into this category. Some Americans believe they have the right to own guns to protect themselves. Other Americans believe that only police officers or people in the military should be allowed to carry guns.

On the board, write:

CONFLICT CAN OCCUR BETWEEN:

1. Individuals
2. Groups
3. Countries

Activity: Identifying The Type Of Conflict

Purpose: The purpose of this activity is to help students identify the sources and causes of their personal conflicts and categorize them into *possessions/resources* or *values/needs.*

Materials Needed/Preparation: None

Introduce the activity by saying:

A conflict can be between individuals. In other words, there can be a conflict between you and one other person. Raise your hand if you are currently having a conflict with another person. (Pause for responses.) *Those of you with your hands raised, please stand if you want to tell us whether your conflict is about possessions and resources or values and needs. Do not name the person with whom you are in conflict. If you are unsure what type of conflict you are having, we will ask the class to decide.*

Have the students who are standing describe their conflicts. Then continue the lesson by saying:

Some conflicts are about possessions and resources <u>and</u> *values and needs. For example, if your brother or sister constantly comes into your room and messes with your stuff and laughs and teases you when you ask him or her to stop, this is an example of both types of conflict. You feel you own your room (possessions and resources) and that your brother or sister does not have the right (values and needs) to come into your room without your permission. Your brother or sister may feel you do __not__ own the room (possessions and resources) and that because you are not the parent, you can't tell him or her what to do (values and needs). This is a combo conflict—a combination of number one (possessions and resources) and number two (values and needs).*

Conflicts can also arise between groups of people. Democrats and Republicans, the two main political groups in the United States, are often in conflict over how to run the country. Conflict can occur between special-interest groups, such as environmentalists and developers. When a company is interested in building a new shopping mall or housing development in a rural area, these two groups are often in conflict about how much land can be developed without destroying the community's natural environment.

Activity and Activity Sheet: What Groups Do I Belong To?

Purpose: The purpose of this activity is to make students more aware of the interactions they regularly have with various groups of people.

Materials Needed/Preparation: Make a copy of *What Groups Do I Belong To?* (page 20) for each student.

Begin the activity by distributing the activity sheet and a pencil to each student. Tell the students to read the descriptions of the different groups listed on the activity sheet and circle those to which they belong.

Continue the activity by saying:

Students often participate in more groups than they realize. The more people you come into contact with, the more potential there is for conflict. Let's look at all the different groups you may belong to. I am going to call out eight categories of groups. If you are a member of any of the categories I name, please stand. Keep track of the number of times you stand. Each of you will stand at least once. Some of you may stand eight times!

Please stand if you:

1. *currently play or are signed up to play on a sports team this season*
2. *attend a church, synagogue, witness hall, mosque, or temple*
3. *belong to a club such as Boy Scouts or Girl Scouts, fan club, chess club, science club, 4-H club, etc.*
4. *attend an after-school program*
5. *live in a neighborhood that has a name, such as* (CALL OUT NAMES OF NEIGHBORHOODS THAT FEED INTO THE SCHOOL)

6. *belong to a group of relatives who hold family reunions every year or every other year*
7. *always hang out with the same group of friends*
8. *attend a public school* (<u>CHANGE TO PRIVATE SCHOOL IF APPROPRIATE</u>)

Have the students raise their hands to indicate how many times they stood.

Continue the lesson by saying:

Many of you mix with lots of different people during the week. Raise your hand if you are currently having a conflict within one of these groups. If you would like to, please tell the class if the group conflict you are involved with is about possessions and resources (#1), values and needs (#2), or both (#1 and #2).

Countries can be in conflict with one another, and these conflicts often result in war. Some countries have been in conflict with one another for many years. Countries typically argue over the location of the borders of their territory (possessions/resources) and what type of government they should have (values/ needs). Can anyone tell me what countries are currently in conflict with one another? Raise your hand if you can. (Accept any correct answer.)

Even if we are not directly involved, we may be drawn into a personal or individual conflict or surrounded by it through our association or contact with different people or groups or by living in a country that is in conflict with another country. None of us lives alone on an island. And because we have contact with people, the potential for conflict exists. It is important to learn how to deal with conflict in a positive way.

Experiment: Baking Soda And Vinegar

Purpose: The purpose of this experiment is to give students a visual image of conflict and to relate conflict to physical symptoms.

Materials Needed/Preparation: You will need a bottle with a cork, vinegar, and a spoonful of baking soda. Pour the vinegar into the glass bottle until the bottle is about $3/4$ full. Carefully add one spoonful of baking soda, then quickly cork the bottle. The baking soda and vinegar will react instantly, pop the cork off the bottle, and foam down the sides of the bottle.

Introduce the experiment by saying:

A lot of you have already seen this experiment with baking soda and vinegar. Who can tell me what happens when these two chemicals come into contact with one another? (Pause for responses.)

That's right. The two chemicals rub each other the wrong way, and they explode. How many of you know someone who makes you feel like you are going to explode? (Pause for responses.)

The trick is learning how not to explode or not to pop. Wherever we go, we will encounter annoying people or annoying situations. We will get mad at others, and we will have conflict in our lives. But we can control how intense the anger and conflict will be. Anger and conflict are not necessarily bad things, but we must learn how to get along with everyone in spite of our differences.

Experiment: Oil And Water

Purpose: The purpose of this experiment is to show students that some chemical reactions are not explosive and to encourage students to aim for a similarly harmonious coexistence with people who rub them the wrong way.

Materials Needed/Preparation: You will need a glass bottle with a screw-on cap, water, blue food coloring, and oil. Pour the water into the glass bottle until it is full. Add enough blue food coloring to make the water visible. Fill the remaining half of the bottle with oil. Screw the cap onto the bottle. Shake the bottle several times. The water and oil will separate.

Introduce the experiment by saying:

Let me show you another experiment. I will add water to the bottle until the bottle is half-full. Then I will add food coloring to make the water easier to see. Now I will fill the rest of the bottle with oil. When I shake the bottle, what happens? (Pause for responses.) *Yes, the two chemicals mix with one another, but they do not explode. Notice how the two elements settle out after a few minutes. In other words, these two chemicals have opposite properties and do not mix, but they are able to get along in a small space without popping or exploding.*

Like this bottle of oil and water, each of us must learn how to get along with people who are different from us. The key is learning how to get along with people we do not like. We can all get along with our friends. It is learning to get along with our enemies that is a challenge.

Some people think that if you do not like someone, it is OK to treat that person with disrespect and tease or mock him or her. This is not true. You can be civil and courteous to people you do not care for. As an adult, I am expected to work with people who are not necessarily my friends. I may not like them, but I can work alongside them and get the job done.

Demonstration: Poppers [1]

Purpose: The purpose of the demonstration is to relate the varying degrees of popping levels among a group of tennis balls to the students' individual popping levels or reactions to conflict.

Materials Needed/Preparation: You will need purchased poppers or three tennis balls, preferably of different colors, and scissors or a sharp knife. Cut the tennis balls in half and turn them inside out. These are your *poppers.* You want three different rates of poppers—slow, medium, and fast. The popper rate can be adjusted by the number of times the poppers are turned inside out and bent in half. The more pliable the popper, the longer the pop time. The more rigid the popper, the more immediate the response time.

Begin the demonstration by laying three poppers on a table in the front of the classroom. Then say:

> *I brought along something to show you today.* (Hold up the poppers.) *These are poppers. They are made of rubber and look like balls cut in half. When you turn them inside out and lay them on a table, they pop up. Like people, poppers come in different sizes and colors. You can't tell by looking which ones will pop quickly and which ones will pop slowly.* (Demonstrate how quickly each popper pops.) *The popper that took the longest to pop was the one I spent the most time turning inside out. The reason I did that is because the more you bend the popper, the more flexible it becomes and the slower it is to pop. That's true of people, too. The more flexible and easygoing you are, the less often your temper will explode.*

Activity Sheet: My Rate Of Popping

Purpose: The purpose of this activity is to have students evaluate their own rate of popping.

Materials Needed/Preparation: Make a copy of *My Rate Of Popping* (page 21) for each student.

Begin the activity by distributing the activity sheet to each student. Then say:

> *Raise your hand if you believe you get angry very quickly.* (Pause for responses.) *How many of you feel that your popping rate is medium to average?* (Pause for responses.) *How many of you are slow to pop?* (Pause for responses.)
>
> *Knowing what kind of popper you are is the first step in learning to resolve conflict.*
>
> *In addition to knowing your rate of popping, it helps to know what kinds of things are likely to cause you to pop. If you get really upset when your brother calls you*

---

1. Taken from: Cobb, Vicki and Darling, Kathy. *Bet You Can! Science Possibilities To Fool You.* New York, NY: HarperTrophy, 1989

names, for example, name-calling would be one of your poppers. It is not un-usual for a person to have several poppers.

It is interesting that we know what other people's poppers are and sometimes we use knowing this to our advantage. When we do that, we say we know how to push that person's buttons. Years ago, I knew a student who was a huge fan of a particular college sports team. Whenever that team lost, other students at the school would say the team was a loser, that it stunk, and make other remarks that were not very nice. This would violently upset the student I am talking about. He would yell and scream and be sent to the office. The other students made this happen on purpose every season. They did it because they knew what this student's poppers were and could use what they knew against him to get him into trouble.

Raise your hand if you think you know what the popper of someone in your family is. (Pause for responses.)

Raise your hand if you have sometimes set that person's popper off on purpose to annoy him or her. (Pause for responses.)

When someone sets your popper off, who is in control of the situation? You or the person who knows what your popper is and is using that knowledge against you? (Pause for responses.)

You are in charge, because you are the only person you can control and the only person who can control you. You can control your temper. That doesn't mean that you won't get angry or upset when someone uses your popper. It does mean that when that happens, you do not have to explode like the baking soda and vinegar.

Look at your activity sheet. With #1 meaning being slow to pop and #10 meaning being very quick to pop, circle the number that matches your rate of popping.

Activity Sheet: My Physical Signs

Purpose: The purpose of this activity sheet is to give each student an opportunity to list three physical signs that occur when he/she is angry.

Materials Needed/Preparation: Make a copy of *My Physical Signs* (page 22) for each student.

Distribute the activity sheet to each student. Then introduce the activity sheet by saying:

Write down at least three physical reactions that happen inside your body when you get angry. Make sure you write down only what is going on inside your body. Sometimes students list what they do after they get mad, like throwing some-

thing or yelling. Those are examples of actions that occur outside the body. I want you to list reactions that occur inside the body. When you have finished, please turn your paper in to me. (Allow time for the students to complete the task.)

Some students have told me they do not know what is happening inside them because they have never thought about it. If you feel that way, here is a homework project: The next time you get mad, pay attention to your body's reactions and list them on a piece of paper.

Next time I come in, I will show you a poster listing the top three responses. (Collect the papers and make a poster listing the students' responses. Save the list for Lesson 2. If you are presenting this unit in more than one class, say that you will also bring in the results from those classes. Then ask the students: *How many of you think that everybody's answers will be about the same? How many think the answers will be different? How many do not know what to expect?*)

Activity Sheet: What Are My Poppers?

Purpose: The purpose of this activity sheet is to give each student an opportunity to list three things that make him/her angry.

Materials Needed/Preparation: Make a copy of *What Are My Poppers?* (page 24) for each student. Optional: Make a transparency of *Anger Mountain* (page 23).

Distribute the activity sheet to each student. Then introduce the activity sheet by saying:

*Becoming aware of your weak spots or poppers puts you in control of your temper and helps resolve conflict. I want you to think about three things that are your poppers and write each one on your activity sheet. These things should be things that really get to you. Don't list a name like **my sister** or **brother**. List only the behavior or action that makes you pop. Please turn your papers in to me when you have finished.* (Allow time for the students to complete the task Collect the papers and make a poster listing the students' responses. Save the list for Lessons 2 and 6.)

While the students are working, draw on the board a picture like the one to the right. (Note: You may also use a transparency of *Anger Mountain* [page 25] for this activity.)

Continue the lesson by saying:

This is a picture of Anger Mountain. When you are at the top of the mountain, you are very angry. But before you get to the top, physical changes happening inside your body let you know you are getting annoyed or frus-

trated. Maybe your fist clenches. Your ears ring. Your heart races. You start talking. Your head pounds. Or maybe something else happens. (As you name the possibilities, show them going up the mountain as illustrated to the right.)

A physical reaction takes place when your temper rises, and it is very important for you to be able to identify these physical signs and recognize them. Sometimes we may say things in our minds that make us even more angry. Things such as, "That's not fair," or "I can't stand this."

The physical signs we experience are like steps taking us up Anger Mountain. We do not have to climb all the way to the mountain top. If we pay attention to the steps or physical signs along the way, we can turn around and return to the foot of the mountain.

Lesson 1 Summary: How To Stop Before You Pop

Conclude the lesson by saying:

In this lesson, we looked at the two sources of conflict. We learned about the types of conflicts we most often encounter in our daily lives. What are they? (Possession/Resources or Values/Needs)

We also learned that conflict is everywhere. Conflict occurs between individuals, groups, and countries. Conflict touches each of us in some way.

Conflict may make us feel completely out of control. Before that feeling overcomes us, we experience physical reactions or signs. Once we become aware of the physical signs associated with conflict and pay attention to them, we can control our angry feelings.

It is OK to have conflict. It is not OK to explode and harm others or yourself while you are in conflict. When I did the science experiment involving baking soda and vinegar, we saw the two chemicals come into contact and explode and erupt in a violent way. I did another experiment, with oil and water. In contrast to the baking soda and vinegar, this experiment taught us that it is possible for two different chemicals to come into contact with one another and coexist peacefully. We know it is also possible for people to come into contact with each other and coexist peacefully.

What Groups Do I Belong To?

NAME _____   DATE_____

Directions: Look at the list of groups below. Circle all the ones that you belong to.

1. Currently play or are signed up to play on a sports team

2. Attend a church, synagogue, witness hall, mosque, or temple

3. Belong to a club such as Boy Scouts or Girl Scouts,
    chess, scrabble, science, 4-H, etc.

4. Attend an after-school program

5. Live in a neighborhood that has a name

6. Belong to a group of relatives who hold family reunions every year or every other year

7. Always hang out with the same group of friends

8. Attend a public, private, or parochial school

Total number of groups I am in _____.

HOW TO STOP BEFORE YOU POP © 2007 MAR★CO PRODUCTS, INC. 1-800-448-2197

My Rate Of Popping

NAME _____ DATE_____

Directions: Everyone has a different rate of popping. On the chart below, rate your popping point.

My Physical Signs

NAME _____   DATE_____

Directions: List three physical signs
you experience before you pop.

POP

#1

#2

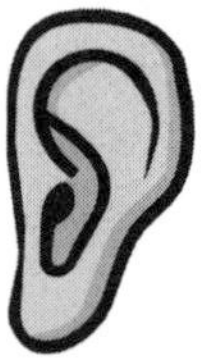

RINGING

#3

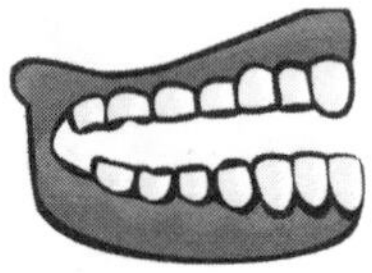

GRINDING

RACING

Anger Mountain

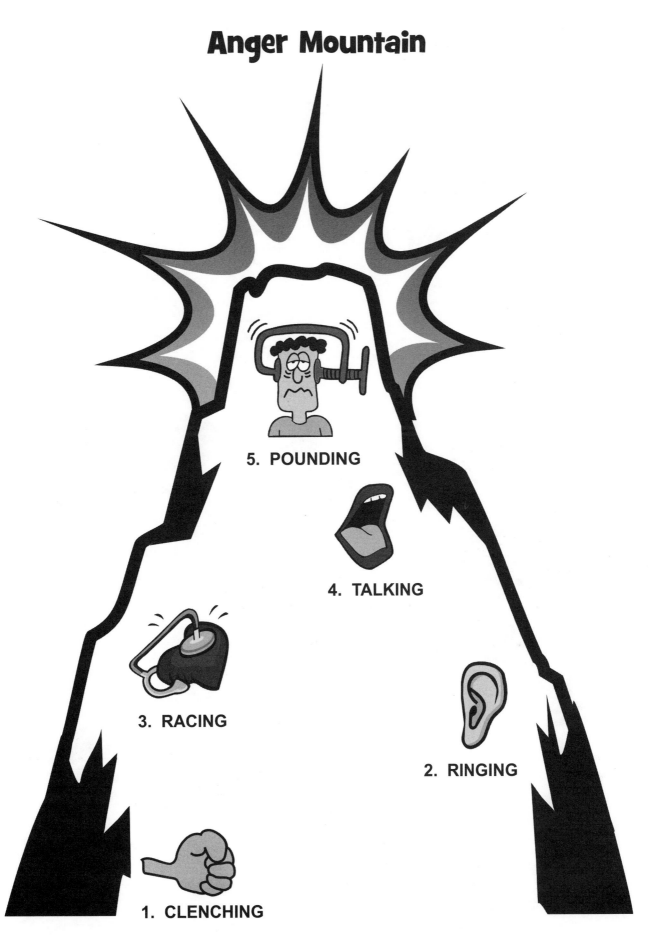

What Are My Poppers?

NAME _____ DATE_____

POP

Directions:
List your three
top poppers.

POP

POP

LESSON 2
Find Your Balance

Materials Needed:

For the leader:
- ☐ Posters from Lesson 1 (summary of one or more classes' poppers and physical signs)
- ☐ Commercial Tornado Tube, 2 large plastic bottles, and red food coloring
  or
  Glass jar with lid, food coloring, water, dishwashing detergent for homemade tornado
- ☐ Chalkboard and chalk or white board and markers
- ☐ 1 light green wiggle-shaped balloon, 1 dark green wiggle-shaped balloon, and permanent marker for *Turtle Balloon* (page 34)
  or
  Turtle Sock Puppet Pattern (pages 35-37), green cardstock, black marker, green sock, stapler, staples, glue, and wiggly eyes (optional)
  or
  Purchased turtle (stuffed animal or puppet)

For each student:
- ☐ Copy of *Tornado* (page 32)
- ☐ Copy of *How I Get Balanced* (page 33)
- ☐ Copy of *Penny Experiment Reactions* (page 38)
- ☐ Plastic bag containing 5 pennies
- ☐ Pencil
- ☐ Crayons or markers

Optional items for purchase:
- ☐ Two-tornado tube ordered through National School Products, 101 East Broadway. Maryville, TN 37804. 1-800-627-9393. www.NationalSchoolProducts.com

Lesson:

Introduce the lesson by saying:

At our last meeting, you listed the three things that make you the most mad in the shortest amount of time. You also listed the physical signs that go on inside your body when you first start to feel anger. I have listed your top responses on posters for us to discuss. (*Note*: If presenting this unit in more than one class, include the results from all classes on the poster. Then ask the students: What do the classes have in common? What differences do you see? Do you think we would get the same answers if we asked students at another grade level? At another school?)

Experiment: Tornado Tube [2]

Purpose: The purpose of this experiment is to show how angry feelings are like a tornado.

Materials Needed/Preparation: If you are using a commercial Tornado Tube, fill one large plastic bottle with water. Add red food coloring. Fit the other bottle on top of this one, connected to it by a tornado tube. Turn the bottle upside down. Swirl it to get the tornado effect.

If you are not using a commercial Tornado Tube, you can create your own tornado in a jar. Fill a glass jar about ¾ full of water. Add 1 teaspoon of dishwashing detergent and 1 drop of food coloring. Shake the bottle roughly for about 30 seconds. Give the lid a quick twist.

Begin the experiment by placing the Tornado Tube where all the students can see it. Then say:

You can see from the posters that the same things tend to annoy all of us or make us angry. A lot of the answers describe poppers that are a lot alike. The same thing is true for the physical signs associated with anger. When some of these things are happening to you, you may feel like you have a tornado inside your body.

Conduct the experiment. Then continue the lesson by saying:

Just like what's happening inside the bottles, you feel a tornado that is raging out of control is rushing around inside you.

I put food coloring in the water to make the tornado easier to see. Why do you think I used red food coloring? (The color red is sometimes used to show anger; a person's face may get red when he/she is angry; in the bullring, the red cape attracts the bull and makes him angry; and any other appropriate answers.)

There are some things you can do to help you calm down before you reach the tornado stage. That doesn't mean you won't get angry or that you should pretend not to be angry. It means that when you control your anger, or your tornado, you can seek a solution rather than just explode or pop. When you control your temper, you get your temper to work <u>for</u> you rather than <u>against</u> you.

Activity Sheet: Tornado

Purpose: The purpose of this activity sheet is to encourage the students think about how they react when they are angry.

Materials Needed/Preparation: Make a copy of *Tornado* (page 32) for each student.

---

2. Taken from: Making a homemade tornado. Reeko's Mad Scientist Lab. http://www.spartechsoftware.com/reeko/Experiments/ExpTornado.htm

Distribute the activity sheet, crayons or markers, and a pencil to each student. Then introduce the activity sheet by saying:

On the activity sheet, please place a checkmark next to the tornado that best describes you. Then list the main reasons or causes for this tornado. Color the tornado with whatever color best fits the feeling associated with your tornado. You may use whatever color you wish.

Activity: Temper

Purpose: The purpose of this activity is to give the students an opportunity to evaluate the situations that make them angry.

Materials Needed/Preparation: None

Introduce the activity by saying:

I am going to read aloud some statements about anger. If you have ever had thoughts like these or done any of the things I describe, please stand.

1. *Stand if you have embarrassed yourself or someone else by losing your temper.*

2. *Stand if you have ever said something in anger that you wished you could take back.*

3. *Stand if you have ever gotten into major trouble at home or at school because of your temper.*

4. *Stand if you have ever broken something in anger that you wish you hadn't destroyed.*

5. *Stand if losing your temper has made things worse rather than better.*

If you stood when I read any of these statements, losing your temper is not working for you. In other words, losing your temper is not getting you what you want or need. It is OK to be angry or to have a temper. But you have to learn to control your temper, not lose it. Once the tornado of angry feelings starts swirling around inside you, it may be impossible to control your temper or predict what will happen when you lose it.

I have heard people say they have bad tempers they can't control. If you can't control yourself, no one else can. People may say they <u>can't</u> control their tempers when they really mean they <u>won't</u> control them. Controlling your temper is a choice, not a reflex.

Presentation: Yin Yang

Purpose: The purpose of this presentation is to teach students how to balance their anger with a calming force.

Materials Needed/Preparation: On the board, draw a Yin Yang symbol (see illustration to right).

Begin the presentation by pointing to the symbol on the board. Then ask the students:

> *How many of you have seen this symbol before?* (Accept all appropriate responses.)

> *What does it mean?* (Accept all appropriate responses.)

Continue the presentation by saying:

> *The Yin Yang is an ancient Chinese symbol. It represents the balance of forces or equilibrium. In our case, it means the quest to balance our tempers with a calming force so we can harness our anger to our benefit.*

> *Think about the tornado experiment. When the water in the bottle was smooth, it was the opposite of when it was in the tornado state. Think about your own Yin Yang as we learn ways to find balance in our lives.*

Activity Sheet: How I Get Balanced

Purpose: The purpose of this activity sheet is to have the students identify the things, activities, or people that help create balance in their lives.

Materials Needed/Preparation: Make a copy of *How I Get Balanced* (page 33) for each student.

Distribute the activity sheet to each student. Then introduce the activity sheet by saying:

> *Think about things in your life that give you a sense of balance or calm you down. Some people may find balance through being with a person or a pet or in an activity such as listening to music, playing sports, eating a certain food, sleeping, reading a book or magazine, playing computer or board games, or watching television.* (Allow time for the students to complete their activity sheets.)

Have the students share their completed activity sheets by naming the things they listed. Summarize their contributions by writing their answers on the board.

Activity: Turtle Balloon And Balancing Activity

Purpose: The purpose of this activity is to create a classroom mascot.

Materials Needed/Preparation: The mascot is made of balloons (page 34) or you may make a turtle sock puppet (pages 35-37). The mascot remains in the room as a visual reminder of the lesson. A commercial turtle puppet or stuffed animal may also be used.

Introduce the activity by saying:

> *I am making (have brought) a mascot for the classroom. Can anyone guess what would be a good mascot to remind us of what we have learned about calming down and controlling our tempers?* (Pause for responses.)

> *I thought of a turtle. Why would a turtle be a good mascot?* (The turtle is a slow-moving animal, and it will remind us to slow down when something makes us angry.)

> (If you are making the turtle balloon, use this sentence) *While I am making the turtle, I want to teach you a few ways to calm yourself down.*

> (If you are using something other than the turtle balloon, use this sentence.) *I want to teach you a few ways to calm yourself down.*

> *I want everyone to take three deep breaths. When you take a deep breath, your stomach expands and the knot you may feel in your stomach when you are angry goes away. After you take three deep breaths, count to 10 slowly. I always put a long word like Mississippi between the numbers to stretch the counting out even more. We will do both things together as a group, taking deep breaths and counting to 10.*

Lead the students in the activity. Then say:

> *When you are at school, you may not be able to do some of the things you listed on your activity sheet that help you find balance. But you can always do the deep breathing and counting and visualize doing what you would like to be doing or being with a person who makes you feel calm.*

Presentation: Movements

Purpose: The purpose of this presentation is to teach the students about popular movements that initiated change through lawful procedures.

Materials Needed/Preparation: None

Explain *movements* by saying:

Many movements in the United States have come about because people were angry or frustrated with the way things were. These people were able to harness their anger and use it to change society by changing laws or policies. The Civil Rights Movement; the Women's Suffrage Movement, which gave women the right to vote; and Mothers Against Drunk Driving are examples of peaceful movements that brought about change through new laws or policies. The people involved in these movements used their anger to their advantage and made things better for all of us. These reactions to anger are examples of the opposites represented by the Yin Yang symbol. We also have examples of cases in which people who were angry with the way things were hurt people or damaged things in order to release their frustration. Some examples of this would be terrorist attacks or hostage situations.

Experiment And Activity Sheet: Penny Experiment Reactions

Purpose: The purpose of this experiment is to have students experience frustration and react to it calmly.

Materials Needed/Preparation: Each student will need a plastic bag containing 5 pennies. Make a copy of *Penny Experiment Reactions* (page 38) for each student.

Distribute a plastic bag of pennies and an activity sheet to each student. Then introduce the experiment by saying:

In a few minutes, we are going to conduct an experiment. This experiment may be frustrating for some of you. If you get frustrated, I want you to use some of the calming strategies we practiced earlier. The calming strategies include taking three deep breaths, counting to 10, and visualizing being with a person or being involved in an activity that gives you balance.

After you do the experiment, please complete the activity sheet. List your level of frustration and how effectively the calming strategies helped you find balance so you could complete the experiment.

I gave each of you a plastic bag containing five pennies. When I say, "Start," take the pennies out of the bag. You will then try to balance the pennies on their edges. Do not prop the pennies on anything. They must be freestanding. You will have _____ minutes to complete this experiment. If you are able to balance all five pennies on your table/desk, raise your hand. I will call your name and then collect your pennies from you. Watch while I demonstrate with one penny what you are to do. (Try to balance one penny on its edge. You may not be able to do it! If you can't, admit that it is difficult. But encourage the students to give it a try.) *Are there any questions before we start?* (Pause for questions.) *You may begin.*

When the allotted time has elapsed, tell those students who haven't already started to fill out the activity sheet to do so. When everyone has completed the activity sheet, ask:

How many of you found this frustrating?

How many found it was easy?

How many found it so/so?

How effective were the calming strategies in helping you find balance?

Then say:

This was just an experiment, so it should not have made you too angry. The frustration this experiment might have made you feel is not the same as the anger level caused by the poppers you listed earlier. Practice using calming strategies with low poppers. That will help you calm down when you face high poppers.

Lesson 2: Summary: Balance

Conclude the lesson by saying:

In this lesson, we looked at balance. When we are out of balance because of conflict, we may feel like we have a tornado brewing inside us. Before the tornado overcomes us completely, we can find balance by paying attention to physical signs.

We have a turtle mascot to remind us to slow down. We have discussed different things that create a sense of calm. Using these calming strategies lets us control the tornado so the tornado is not controlling us.

Some important movements have come about because people were angry and wanted things to change. Conflict and anger can make good things happen when they are expressed in an appropriate way.

During our penny experiment on frustration, you had a chance to use calming strategies to help you accomplish a task.

Tornado

NAME _____ DATE_____

Directions: Place a checkmark next to the *tornado feeling* that best describes you and list the main causes or reasons why this is true.

☐ I have never felt like I have a tornado inside.

☐ I sometimes feel like I have a tornado inside.

☐ I often feel like I have a tornado inside.

☐ I always feel like I have a tornado inside.

The main reasons I have *tornado feelings* are _____

_____

Color the tornado below with a color that best fits your *tornado feelings*. Then tell why you picked that color.

I picked this color because _____

_____

How I Get Balanced

NAME _____ DATE_____

Directions: List all the activities, people, or things that help you keep balance in your life.

_____   _____

_____   _____

_____   _____

_____   _____

_____   _____

_____   _____

_____   _____

_____   _____

Turtle Balloon Mascot Instructions

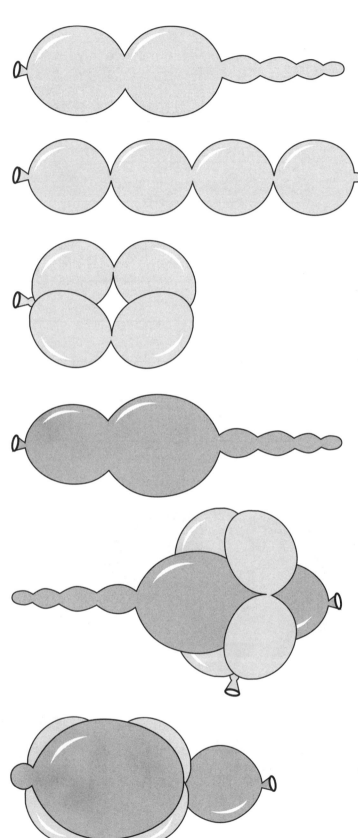

Materials Needed/Preparation:
- ☐ 1 large light green wiggly-shaped balloon
- ☐ 1 large dark green wiggly-shaped balloon
- ☐ Permanent marker

Directions:

Blow up two wiggly-shaped balloons and release the air so the balloons are stretched out and pliable.

Bow up the light green wiggly balloon. Release the air so that only the first two sections have air in them.

To form feet, twist the two sections with air in them into four balls. Twist about five times so the feet are secure. Be sure to leave a small section of the balloon un-filled with air. You will need to do this so you can tie a knot.

Tie the balloon ends together. The balloon will form a sort of square.

Bow up the dark green wiggly balloon. Release the air so that only the first two sections have air in them. These sections will be the turtle's head and body.

Push the second balloon (head and body) through the middle of the square made by the first balloon (feet). Twist the second balloon around two of the feet to make the head.

Lay the body of the turtle over the opening of the square. Tie the ends of the second and first balloons together to form a tail.

Using a permanent marker, draw the turtle's face and shell on the second balloon.

Turtle Sock Puppet Pattern

Materials Needed:
- ☐ Green cardstock
- ☐ Green sock
- ☐ Black marker
- ☐ Stapler and staples
- ☐ Scissors
- ☐ Glue
- ☐ Wiggly eyes (optional)

Directions: [3]

Reproduce the pattern pieces on green cardstock. Glue the feet and tail to the turtle's shell. Staple the sides of the turtle's shell and belly together. The sock is inserted between the turtle's shell and belly. Draw a face on the sock and, using glue, add the wiggly eyes (optional).

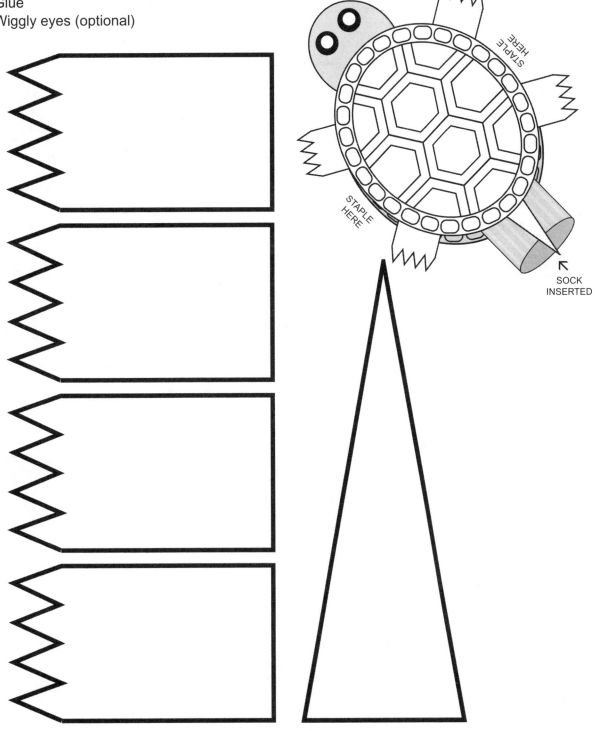

STAPLE HERE

STAPLE HERE

SOCK INSERTED

---

3. Adapted from: http://www.gma.org/turtles/sock.html

Turtle Shell Pattern

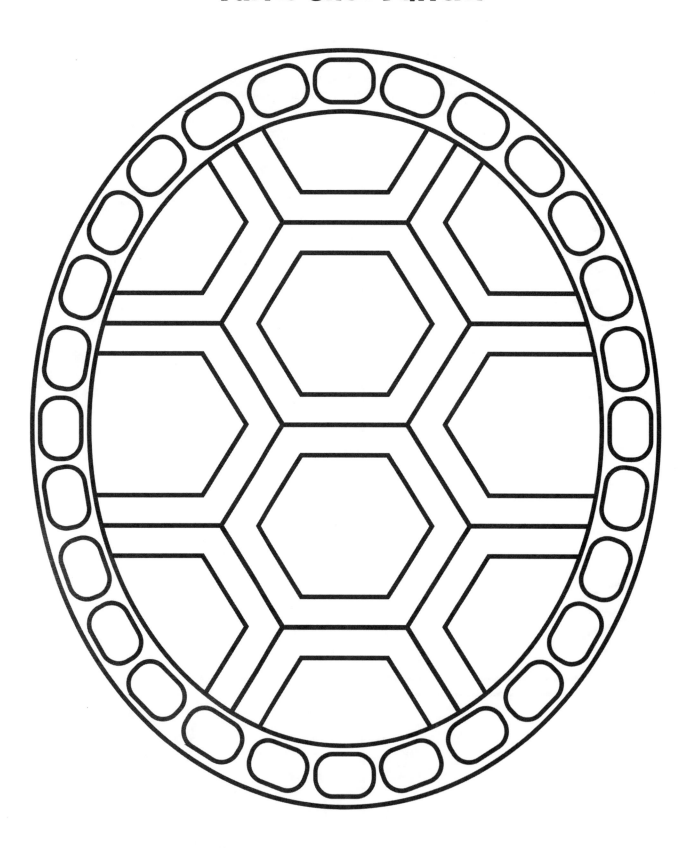

HOW TO STOP BEFORE YOU POP © 2007 MAR*CO PRODUCTS, INC. 1-800-448-2197

Turtle Belly Pattern

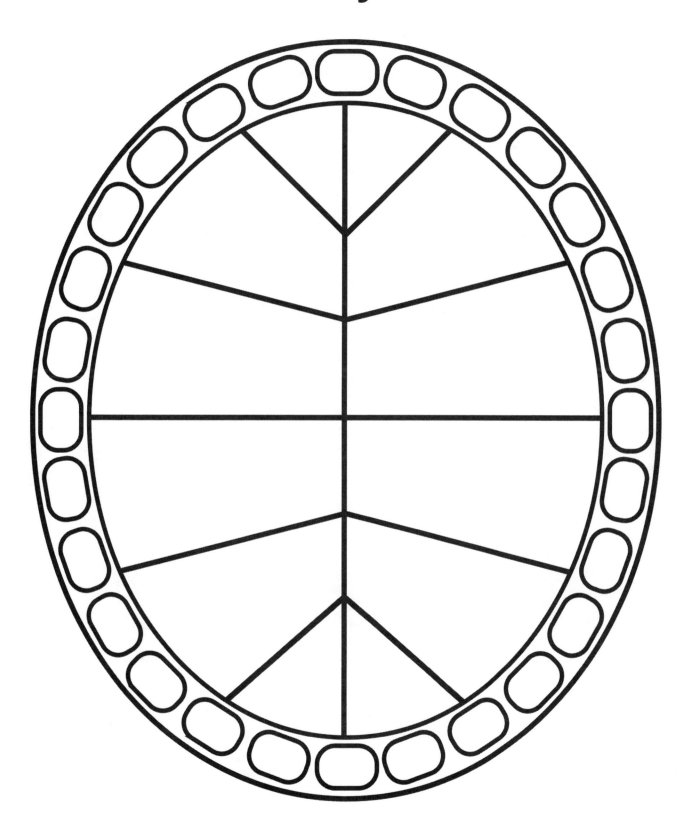

Penny Experiment Reactions

NAME _____   DATE_____

Directions: Rate your level of frustration and circle that number.

1 ···· 2 ···· 3 ···· 4 ···· 5 ···· 6 ···· 7 ···· 8 ···· 9 ···· 10

LOW   HIGH

Directions: Rate how effective your calming strategies were and circle that number.

1 ···· 2 ···· 3 ···· 4 ···· 5 ···· 6 ···· 7 ···· 8 ···· 9 ···· 10

LOW   HIGH

38

Power

Materials Needed:

For the leader:
- ☐ Chalkboard and chalk or white board and markers
- ☐ Container
- ☐ Clock with a second hand
- ☐ *Puppet Pattern* (page 48)
- ☐ Blank piece of 8½" x 11" paper
- ☐ Crayons or markers

For each student:
- ☐ Copy of *Who Has Power?* (page 45)
- ☐ Copy of *Feeling Stories* (page 46)
- ☐ Copy of *Power Test* (page 47)
- ☐ Pencil
- ☐ Piece of scrap paper
- ☐ Blank piece of 8½" x 11" paper
- ☐ Crayons or markers

Lesson:

Introduce the lesson by saying:

Power *is an important concept associated with learning to express and gain control over your anger. I am not talking about electrical, nuclear, or solar power. I am talking about* people power. *People with power have the authority to tell you and/or others what to do.*

Activity Sheet: Who Has Power

Purpose: The purpose of this activity sheet is for students to list 10 living people whom they believe have power.

Materials Needed/Preparation: Make a copy of *Who Has Power?* (page 45) for each student.

Distribute the activity sheet and a pencil to each student. Have the students complete the activity sheet. Then ask:

Can anyone tell us who has power in the world?

Write the students' answers on the board. Then summarize their answers by grouping the names mentioned into categories such as political leaders, sport figures, celebrities, etc.

Continue the lesson by saying:

When we think of ways to channel our tempers into more positive directions, we have the power to do so.

On the board, I have listed the names of many powerful people. We are going to focus on one person who has a lot of power—you. Kids often think they do not have power because there are so many people telling them what to do—coaches, parents, teachers, older brothers and sisters, and so on. So what kind of power do you think I am talking about? (Pause for responses.) *The kind of power I am talking about is the power you have over what you think and the power you have over your emotions.*

Sometimes we give our power away without realizing it. We may let other people decide how we should act or think. We may let other people control our feelings by what we tell ourselves about a situation. For example, the expression "you are putting me in a bad mood" means your mood is controlled by someone other than you. Is that really possible? It is your own thoughts that are creating the bad mood. You have the power not someone else.

I am going to read eight common expressions. If you have ever made a statement like one I read or if you have ever thought that way, I want you to stand up. Do not talk, just stand up. Then sit down until I read another statement that sounds like something you have said or felt. Keep track of how many times you stand.

Read the following statements about giving power away:

They really get on my nerves!
She/he drives me nuts!
I can't help it.
I have a bad temper.
I can't stand how he/she acts.
She/he makes me so mad!
They really make me sick!
He/she started it!

Tell the students to count the number of times they stood. Then say:

The more times you stood, the more times you have given your power away. When you are making these kinds of statements or thinking these kinds of thoughts, you are letting other people decide how you will feel. You are giving your power to others rather than keeping it for yourself.

40

If you are making these statements or thinking these thoughts, you are giving your power away. Other people are deciding whether your day will be good or bad. It is like you are a puppet and other people are controlling your strings. You are not a puppet. You always have control over your thoughts and feelings. When someone hits one of your poppers, you may get so angry that you feel like you have a tornado inside. When this happens, remember that you have power. Visualize the turtle to help you slow down to gain control. When you are in control, you can decide on a solution for the problem and channel your anger in a positive way.

Activity and Activity Sheet:
What You Think Is What You Feel And Feeling Stories

Purpose: The purpose of this activity and activity sheet is to help students realize that what they think will ultimately affect how they feel.

Materials Needed/Preparation: Make a copy of *Feeling Stories* (page 46) for each student. Have each student write his/her name on a piece of scrap paper, fold the paper, and put it into the container.

Distribute the activity sheet to each student. Introduce the activity sheet by writing the following statement on the board:

What you think = What you feel

Then ask:

What do you think this statement means? (Pause for responses.)

When you think positive thoughts, you feel good. When you think negative thoughts, you feel bad. For example: If you think you are stupid and can't do anything right, how do you feel? (Pause for responses.)

Can you be successful when you are feeling that way? (Pause for responses.)

Continue the lesson by saying:

When you have control over your thoughts, you have control over your feelings. To show you what I mean, we are going to do a quick experiment.

Think of three events—one that made you feel sad, one that made you feel scared, and one that made you feel excited. The events have to be things that have really happened to you or that could happen to you in the future. Write each event on your activity sheet. When you have completed the activity sheet, I will pick three names from the container and have those students read aloud what they have written on their activity sheets.

Have the students complete the activity sheet.

Draw three names from the container. Have those students read their stories to the group. Focus on experiences common to many students. For example, if a student describes the death of a pet as his/her sad story, ask the class if anyone else has lost someone he/she loves.

Continue the lesson by saying:

> *Listening to the feeling stories may have reminded you of similar things in your own lives. You may have been reminded of a party, a trip, or a death. When you remembered those things, you may have felt the same feelings you felt when the events actually happened. Did you notice that when your thoughts changed from the scary event to the sad event to the exciting event, your feelings changed, too?* (Pause for responses.) *That is what I meant when I said that what you think equals what you feel.*
>
> *When you are in a situation in which one of your poppers is getting ready to explode, imagine changing your thoughts so your feelings will change, too. Our classroom turtle mascot reminds us to take deep breaths, count to 10, and think of something that gives us a sense of balance. When we do these things, we gain control or get our power back. Once we have our power back, we are in a better position to solve the problem in a positive way.*

Activity Sheet: Power Test

Purpose: The purpose of this activity sheet is to have the students practice strengthening their power.

Materials Needed/Preparation: Make a copy of *Power Test* (page 47) for each student. You will need a clock with a second hand.

Distribute the activity sheet to each student. Introduce the activity sheet by saying:

> *We are going to spend some time strengthening our power. I want you to think of a person, place, or thing (activity or event) that gives you a good feeling inside. This is very similar to what we did when we talked about the Yin Yang. You can choose the same image you did then or pick a different one. I will ask you to focus on your image. I will have you put your heads down and think of this image for one whole minute. There is to be no talking during that minute.*
>
> *This activity is called a* **Power Test.** *Can anyone tell me why?* (Pause for responses.) *It takes power to control your thoughts, but you can do it if you practice. Some of you may not have any trouble thinking of your image for one minute. Others may find that your mind wanders and the time drags. You may find yourself daydreaming. If you have a hard time controlling your thoughts, that may be a*

sign that you are giving your power away. Remember: When you understand that you are the only one who can control your thoughts and feelings, you are on the path to learning how not to pop.

Are there any questions before we begin? (Pause for responses.) *Think of your image. Begin the* **Power Test.**

After one minute, tell the students to stop. Then ask the following questions:

How many of you found this activity easy? Difficult? Why? (Accept all appropriate answers.)

What did you choose to focus on? (person, place, activity, event)

Did any of you think of more than one image? (Accept all appropriate answers.)

Can you think of some times when a **Power Test** *would be helpful?* (Accept all appropriate answers.)

Conclude the activity by saying:

Look at your activity sheet. Indicate how well you were able to focus during that one-minute block of time by circling the appropriate number on the line. Then circle what you thought about during the **Power Test.** *At the bottom of the activity sheet, describe your choice.*

Activity: Paper Hand Puppet [4]

Purpose: The purpose of this activity is to show the students that they are not puppets. They control the puppet. The puppet does not control them.

Materials Needed/Preparation: A sheet of blank 8½ x 11" paper and markers for each student and the leader.

Give each student a piece of blank paper and markers. Using the *Puppet Pattern Directions* (page 48), have the students follow your instructions to make their own puppets. Demonstrate making the puppet as you give the following directions:

Today each of you is going to make a puppet. This is how we are going to do it:

1. *Turn your blank piece of paper lengthwise.*

2-3. *Fold the paper into thirds lengthwise.*

---

4. Taken from: Morgan, Kathleen, Moore, Jo Ellen, and Evans, Joy. *Animal Puppets.* Monterey CA: Evan-Moor Educational Publishers, 1986.

4. *Flip the paper over.*

5. *Fold the paper in half.*

6. *Fold the top edge back so it is even with the crease of the fold.*

7. *Flip the paper over and fold the top edge back so it is even with the crease of the fold.*

8. *Now you will be able to stick your fingers inside the pockets.*

9. *You may bend the corners of the puppet's mouth to create teeth. Use your markers to draw a face on the puppet.*

Continue the activity by saying:

Take a look at your puppet. How will it **move?** (It will move only if you make it move.) *That is right. The puppet does not control you: You control the puppet. You have the power. You are not a puppet controlled by others.*

Lesson 3 Summary: Power

Conclude the lesson by saying:

In this lesson, we learned about power. We may often think we do not have power, but we have power over our thoughts. When we have power over our thoughts, we have power over our feelings.

We listened to three different kinds of stories. And as our thoughts changed, so did our feelings. There is a strong connection between our thoughts and our feelings.

We did a **Power Test** *in which we tried to focus our thoughts, and therefore our feelings, on something positive. When you are faced with a conflict, using the* **Power Test** *strategy will help you gain control.*

We made a simple hand puppet. We are not puppets controlled by others or controlled by our tempers. The puppet reminds us that we are in control of ourselves.

Who Has Power?

Directions: List 10 living people who have power.

1. _____

2. _____

3. _____

4. _____

5. _____

6. _____

7. _____

8. _____

9. _____

10. _____

Feelings Stories

NAME _____ DATE _____

My sad story

_____
_____
_____
_____
_____
_____

My scary story

_____
_____
_____
_____
_____
_____

My exciting story

_____
_____
_____
_____
_____
_____

Power Test

NAME _____   DATE_____

Directions: Rate the *Power Test* on the scale below.

1····2····3····4····5····6····7····8····9····10
SNAP   SO-SO   HARD TO
                                                 FOCUS

Circle what you thought about during the *Power Test.*

person   place   thing

activity   food   trip

past experience   future event

other _____

Describe the thought you circled.

_____

_____

_____

_____

_____

Puppet Pattern

1.

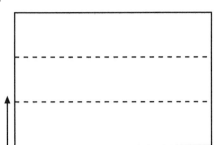

2.

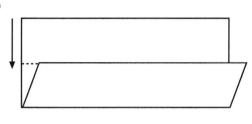

3.

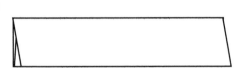

4.

5.

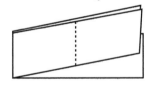

6.

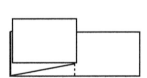

7.

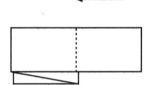

8.

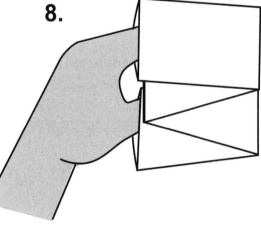

1. Use a 8½" x 11" sheet white copy paper.
2. & 3. Fold the paper into thirds lengthwise.
4. Flip the paper over.
5. Fold the paper in half.
6. Fold the top edge back.
7. Flip the paper over and fold the top edge back.
8. Students may stick their fingers inside the pockets these folds create.

The corners of the puppet's mouth can be bent to create teeth. Decorate the face with crayons or markers.

Body Language

Materials Needed:

For the leader:
- ☐ Chalkboard and chalk or white board and marker
- ☐ Timer or watch with a second hand

For each student:
- ☐ Copy of *Optical Illusion* (page 57)
- ☐ Copy of *Movie Theater Seats* (page 58)
- ☐ Copy of *Elevator Rules* (page 59)
- ☐ Copy of *What Am I Saying?* (page 60)
- ☐ Copy of *Body Language* (page 61)
- ☐ Pencil

Lesson:

Introduce the lesson by saying:

In our lessons so far, we have identified our poppers, focused on our physical reactions to anger, recognized ways to help us calm down and regain our power, and learned that what we <u>think</u> *is what we* <u>feel.</u>

In our next two lessons, we will look at communication skills. When you are in a problematic situation, you need good communication skills to help resolve things. If you are armed with good communication skills, you can solve just about any problem that comes your way. We communicate with others in two different ways: verbally and nonverbally.

Today's lesson will focus on nonverbal behavior. This kind of communication is also called body language. *Does anyone know what that means*? (Pause for responses.) *Body language is how we express ourselves without using words. Some people who study the way people behave believe that half of what we communicate is communicated through body language.*

Activity: Optical Illusion

Purpose: The purpose of this activity is to show the students that nonverbal behaviors can be difficult to read.

Materials Needed/Preparation: Make a copy of *Optical Illusion* (page 57) for each student.

Distribute the activity sheet to each student. Then introduce the activity by saying:

> *Body language is like a hidden message, because it can be hard to read or understand. Look at your* **Optical Illusion** *activity sheet. Stand up if you think you know what message is hidden on the page.*

Allow time for the students to look at the page. Listen to their answers. When everyone has contributed, tell the students the hidden message was "Hello." Congratulate any students who gave that answer.

Continue the activity by saying:

> *Once I told you what the hidden message was, it was easier for some of you to see it. When you look at the picture now, it is pretty easy to see.*
>
> *Like the message on your activity sheet, body language can be hidden. Our body language may be expressing something totally different from the words we are saying. We may say we are not angry, for example, but our body language could be saying that we are. Body language can get in the way when we are trying to resolve a conflict with someone. Our nonverbal behavior might be sending false messages. Or we could be misreading someone else's body language. In other words, body language can be difficult to read, just like the hidden word in our* **Optical Illusion** *activity sheet.*

Demonstration: I'm Sorry

Purpose: The purpose of this activity is to help students understand how facial expressions play a significant role in communication.

Materials Needed/Preparation: On the board, write the words *I'm Sorry*. Underneath the words, draw the faces below.

50

Introduce the demonstration by saying:

Look at the faces on the board. Imagine these are the faces of five different people and that each of those people is saying, "I'm sorry." They use the same words, but their body language, gestures, or facial expressions show that only one really means the words he or she is saying. Which one do you think that is? (Pause for responses.) *For example, have you ever had a friend say he or she is not mad at you, but then ignore you or not talk to you? What did you believe: what your friend said or the way your friend acted?*

Activity Sheets: Movie Theater Seats And Elevator Rules

Purpose: The purpose of this activity is to show students how some nonverbal behaviors can make people very uncomfortable.

Materials Needed/Preparation: Make a copy of *Movie Theater Seats* (page 58) and *Elevator Rules* (page 59) for each student.

Distribute the activity sheets and a pencil to each student. Then introduce the activity sheets by saying:

We learn to communicate through nonverbal behavior at a very young age. In fact, a lot of nonverbal behavior is understood without being taught. Each of the activity sheets you have will show you what I mean.

On your Movie Theater Seats *activity sheet, please circle the place you would sit in the almost-empty movie theater. You will notice that one of the seats is already occupied, so you cannot sit there.*

When the students have finished that task, ask several students where they chose to sit. Then continue the lesson by asking:

How many of you have ever ridden in a crowded elevator? (Pause for responses.) *Think about what it is like to ride in a crowded elevator. On your* Elevator Rules *activity sheet, write down as many rules as you can think of that people tend to follow in a crowded elevator.*

When the students have finished that task, ask:

What elevator rules did you list? (Hands by your side, face the doors, look at the ceiling or the lighted floor, count the floors as you go up or down, be quiet, etc.)

Both elevators and movie theater seats teach us quite a lot about nonverbal behavior.

If you were the one person already sitting in the theater, how would you feel if someone took the seat right next to you? Why? (Pause for responses.)

How would you feel if someone entered a crowded elevator, but faced you instead of turning around to face the doors? Why? (Pause for responses.)

Inappropriate nonverbal behavior can make us feel uncomfortable or weird. When you are trying to resolve a conflict though communication, it is important that your nonverbal behavior put people at ease and make them feel comfortable.

Activity: Can You Read This? [5 & 6]

Purpose: The purpose of this activity is to expose students to communication through body language or nonverbal communication.

Materials Needed/Preparation: None

Introduce the activity by saying:

I am going to show you some gestures commonly used in the United States. I want you to tell me what these gestures mean: [5]

1. Thumbs up (Yes or good job)
2. Thumbs down (No or an unfavorable response)
3. V (Victory or peace sign)
4. Thumb and pointer finger in shape of an *O* (OK)
5. Pointer finger making circles near side of head (Crazy)

Now I want to show you gestures that mean the same thing in many countries. See if you can guess what they mean.

1. Hands together in a prayer position with one side of the face resting on the hands (Asleep)
2. Rubbing stomach (Hungry)
3. Cupping hand to mouth (Thirsty)
4. Rubbing hands together (Cold or excited)
5. Smiling (Happy)

---

5. Sine, Daniela, University of Stirling. *Nonverbal Communication or How Do Our Bodies Talk?* Available at: www.staff.stir.ac.uk/daniela.sime/LectureNVC_for_EUS.html.

6. Imai, Gary. *Gestures: Body Language and Nonverbal Communication.* Curriculum Materials for Grades K-12. Teachers Asian Studies Summer Institute, 1996. Available at: http://www.csupomona.edu/~tassi/gestures.htm.

Sometimes the same gesture means different things in different countries. For example:

1. Putting your thumb and pointer finger in the shape of an *O* means *OK* in the United States. But in France, it means *zero*. And in Japan, it is the sign for money.

2. In the United States, placing your finger on the side of your face means you are undecided about something. In China, that gesture means you are looking down on someone. It is an insult.

3. In the United States, making a fist means you are angry. But in China, a fist is the symbol for the number 10.

Activity Sheet: What Am I Saying?

Purpose: The purpose of this activity sheet is to make students aware of how accurately they interpret nonverbal messages.

Materials Needed/Preparation: Make a copy of *What Am I Saying?* (page 60) for each student.

Distribute the activity sheet to each student. Then introduce the activity sheet by saying:

I am going to give you a short quiz on body language. This quiz will help you see what nonverbal messages you may be sending and help you interpret nonverbal messages people are sending you. The more correct answers you have, the better you are at reading and sending appropriate nonverbal messages.

Read the following references to nonverbal gestures to the students. As you read each reference, have the students perform the gesture. After the students perform each gesture, read the description of the correct gesture (in parentheses). Have those students who correctly performed the gesture place a checkmark next to that gesture on the activity sheet.

1. *Using your arms, show me how you would express victory or reaching a goal.* (upraised arms like a referee in a football game)

2. *Using your arms, how would you show that you are unsure about something or are feeling uncomfortable or awkward?* (fold arms in front of stomach)

3. *Using your fingers, how would you show that you need money?* (place all fingers on the thumb and rub your thumb and fingers together)

4. *Using your hands, how do you show that you have a telephone call?* (extend pinky finger and thumb, close the remaining fingers, place thumb and pointer finger to the side of the face, alongside the ear)

5. **Using your hands and arms, how do you tell someone to get out?** (close fingers into a ball, extend thumb, move hand quickly over one shoulder)

6 **Using your fingers, wish someone good luck.** (cross fingers)

7. **Using your hand, show that you are angry.** (shake a balled fist in the air)

8. **Using your face and hand, show that something smells bad.** (pinch nose with thumb and finger)

Continue the lesson by saying:

Count the number of correct answers you have. The higher the number, the better you are at sending and understanding nonverbal messages. This means that you understand the nonverbal communication of others and send clear nonverbal messages that others can understand. If you have a low score, you may misunderstand nonverbal messages from others and your nonverbal messages may not be clear.

When you are in a conflict situation, faced with one of your main poppers, you may feel like a tornado is brewing inside you. When that happens, you need to visualize two things. One is the turtle mascot, which reminds you to take three deep breaths and count to 10. The second is the Yin Yang, which trains your mind to do something that calms you and helps you maintain balance. Once you have balance, you are ready to communicate. Good communication can help you get through any situation, no matter how difficult. Both verbal and nonverbal communication must be coordinated so that your body language and your words send the same message. When your nonverbal communication and your verbal communication say the same thing, your message will be clear.

When trying to resolve a conflict, the things we do not say (our nonverbal behaviors) may be stumbling blocks. Pay attention to what others are <u>not</u> saying by reading their body language.

How many of you can tell if your mom or dad is angry just by looking at his or her face?

How many of you can tell when your best friend is upset just by glancing at him or her?

If the person you are having a conflict with is sending you strong nonverbal messages that he or she is upset, you may decide to wait until he or she has cooled off before you attempt to solve the problem.

Activity: Mirroring

Purpose: The purpose of this activity is to expose students to a common nonverbal communication technique called *mirroring*. *Mirroring* is believed to enhance communication by putting people at ease and making them feel trusting.

Materials Needed/Preparation: You will need a timer or a watch with a second hand.

Introduce the activity by saying:

> **Mirroring *is one successful body language technique. Mirroring involves imitating the other person's actions or gestures.***
>
> *I am going to assign each of you a partner and have you mirror each other's facial expressions and gestures. Your mirroring should be subtle. That means you shouldn't copy the other person's gestures exactly, but you should use similar gestures. Salespeople find this mirroring technique to be very successful in gaining people's trust. You will mirror your partner for one minute. Then you will switch places and your partner will mirror you.*

Divide the students into pairs, then begin to time them for one minute. After the minute has elapsed, have the partners reverse roles. Time the students for another minute. Then ask:

> *Was this activity easy or difficult? Why?*
>
> *Do you think this is a body language technique you would use?*
>
> *Do you think anyone has ever used this body language technique on you?*

Activity Sheet: Matching Body Language

Purpose: The purpose of this activity sheet is to allow students to apply their knowledge and ability to interpret nonverbal and verbal communication by accurately matching statements to facial expressions.

Materials Needed/Preparation: Make a copy of *Body Language* (page 61) for each student.

Distribute the activity sheet to each student. Then introduce the activity sheet by saying:

> *On the activity sheet, you will find descriptions of body language that students display every day in class. Has your teacher ever caught you daydreaming even though you couldn't figure out how the teacher knew you weren't thinking about math? Teachers are very skilled at reading students' body language. Teachers have a reputation for having "eyes in the back of their heads," but what they really have is a talent for interpreting nonverbal behaviors.*

With your pencil, draw a line from each statement to the facial expression that matches it.

Review the completed activity sheets with the students. The answers are: (a) I'm bored, (b) I'm not listening, (c) I'm in charge, (d) I'm paying attention, (e) I'm confused.

Lesson 4 Summary: Body Language

Conclude the lesson by saying:

We know that in order to resolve a conflict, we need to communicate. There are two ways to communicate—verbally and nonverbally. This lesson looked at non-verbal communication, which is also called body language.

We also learned that we often send nonverbal messages that we are unaware of and that these nonverbal behaviors may block our efforts to resolve the conflict. Looking at the way we communicate through our own body language and reading others' body language accurately can help us restore balance and resolve conflicts.

Optical Illusion

NAME _____ DATE _____

Directions: Look at the picture. Can you see the hidden word?

Movie Theater Seats

NAME _____ DATE_____

Directions: Place an **✗** on the seat you would select in the movie theater. Note that one seat is occupied.

Don't talk during the movie.
Turn your cell phone off or on vibrate. If you need to answer your cell phone, go out to the lobby.
Don't throw trash on the floor.

Elevator Rules

NAME _____ DATE_____

Directions: Write all of the rules you can think of for riding in a crowded elevator.

1. _____

2. _____

3. _____

4. _____

5. _____

6. _____

7. _____

8. _____

What Am I Saying?

NAME _____ DATE_____

Directions: Perform a nonverbal gesture to signify each of the following words. Place a checkmark in the box next to each word whose gesture you perform correctly. When you have finished, count your checkmarks and write the total in the box at the bottom of the page.

☐ 1. victory

☐ 2. uncomfortable

☐ 3. money

☐ 4. phone call

☐ 5. get out

☐ 6. good luck

☐ 7. angry

☐ 8. bad smell

My total number correct ☐

Body Language

NAME _____ DATE_____

Directions: Draw a line from each statement to the facial expression that communicates those words.

I'm paying attention.

I'm not listening.

I'm bored.

I'm in charge.

I'm confused.

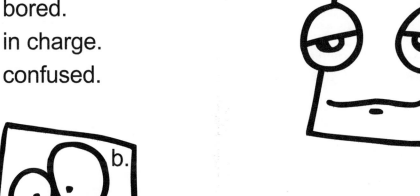

"I" Messages

Materials Needed:

For the leader:
- ☐ 3 pieces of chart paper
- ☐ Marker
- ☐ Tape
- ☐ *Role-Playing Cards* (pages 71-72)
- ☐ Scissors

For each student:
- ☐ Copy of *Message Sending* (page 68)
- ☐ Copy of *"I" Messages* (page 69)
- ☐ Pencil

For each pair of students;
- ☐ Copy of *Role-Play Practice: "I" Messages* (page 70)

Lesson:

Introduce the lesson by saying:

In our last lesson, we learned how to send and read messages nonverbally, through body language.

Today we are going to learn how to communicate verbally through "I" Messages. Does anyone know what "I" Messages are? (Pause for responses.) *"I" Messages are a way to communicate how you are feeling. "I" Messages are clear. When you use an "I" Message, people understand exactly what you are saying. Unlike "I" Messages, nonverbal messages can be mixed, hidden, or misunderstood.*

Activity and Activity Sheet: Message Sending

Purpose: The purpose of this activity and the accompanying activity sheet is to allow students to observe a nonverbal message as it is communicated from one person to another down a line. The focus is on how nonverbal messages may be distorted or misinterpreted.

Materials Needed/Preparation: Make a copy of *Message Sending* (page 68) for each student.

Distribute the activity sheet and a pencil to each student. Introduce the activity by saying:

It is easy for communication to be misinterpreted or misunderstood. This activity shows how this can happen. This activity is similar to a game called Whisper Down The Lane, *in which a message is whispered from one person to the next. How many of you have played this game?* (Pause for responses.)

The difference between this activity and Whisper Down The Lane *is that the message being passed is nonverbal. I will divide you into four groups. There are (<u>NUMBER</u>) students in the class. So (<u>NUMBER OF STUDENTS</u>) divided by four equals (<u>NUMBER</u>). That is the number of students each of the four groups will have.* (Note: If necessary, explain that the groups will not each have the same number of students.)

One group will play at a time. The members of that group will line up with their backs toward me. You will line up this way because I do not want you to see the message being passed down the line until it is your turn to receive the message. The first person in the line will turn toward me, then I will give him or her a series of movements to repeat. The rest of you in line will have your backs turned so you will not see the movements until it is your turn. When it is your turn, you will be tapped on the back or shoulder. When you feel the tap on your shoulder or back, you will turn around to receive the message from the person standing in front of you in the line. If you need to see the message again, you may ask that person to repeat it. After you have received the message, tap the person standing in back of you on the back or shoulder and give him or her the message you have just received. After you pass the message to the next person, return to your seat and sit down.

Each of the four groups will receive five nonverbal gestures and send them down the line. Each person in the line must do his or her best to remember and repeat all five gestures. The group that most accurately repeats all five gestures from the first person in the line to the last person in the line is the group that has done the best job of communicating nonverbally.

Those of you who are seated must remain silent and watch how accurately the message is communicated from person to person. As you observe the activity, record on your activity sheet how accurately the message is given and repeated. Write down your observations without mentioning the names of specific people. Look for patterns or strategies that either help or hurt the group members trying to accurately repeat the gestures. For example, if a student asks to have the message repeated and this helps him or her accurately repeat the message, list this strategy on your activity sheet. Keep track of the number of gestures. It is possible that some gestures or nonverbal behaviors could mistakenly be eliminated or added as the movements are repeated from person to person down the line. Those mistakes would be something to write on the activity sheet. Observing the skills others use successfully may help you when it is your group's turn to pass the message. After we complete the activity, we will have a class discussion about what you noticed.

Show the first person in Group 1 what his/her five gestures are.

Group 1
1. Rub nose with fingers on both hands
2. Place both hands on head
3. Rub tummy with both hands
4. Hold arms straight out and do deep knee bends
5. Stand with both arms raised straight up in the "touchdown" position

Tell Group 1 to begin the activity. When Group 1 has completed the activity, repeat the process with the other three groups.

Group 2
1. Hold one hand up in the "hi" sign
2. Place one hand on top of head
3. Lift one foot
4. Hop in a circle with hand on top of head
5. Shrug shoulders

Group 3
1. Place both hands on shoulders
2. Cross arms over chest and touch shoulders again
3. Shimmy down and up
4. Turn around
5. Rest hands on hips

Group 4
1. Hold arms straight up in a "touchdown" position
2. Sway arms from left to right in the wave
3. With arms out to side, spin around like a helicopter
4. Touch toes
5. Hold both hands up in a "stop" position

When the last group has completed its presentation, instruct the group members to write answers the questions at the bottom of the activity sheet. Then ask the students to refer to their activity sheets as the class discusses the following questions:

What did you notice was happening?

Do you think this happens often? Why?

Did the last group do better than the first group or did each of the groups do equally well?

Did you use any of the strategies you observed when it was your group's turn to pass the message down the line?

Conclude the activity by allowing the students to make any additional contributions from their activity sheet.

"I" Message Format: Presentation

Purpose: The purpose of this presentation is to teach students the meaning of an "I" Message.

Materials Needed/Preparation:

On one piece of chart paper, write:

> I feel (describe how you feel)
> when (describe behavior and stick to the facts)
> because (describe the effects the behavior has on you)

On the second piece of chart paper, write:

> I feel left out and hurt
> when you sit with other people at lunch and ignore me
> because I thought we were friends.

On the third piece of chart paper, write:

> I feel like screaming
> when you act like such a jerk
> because you aren't my friend any more.

Tape the pieces of chart paper to the wall.

Begin the presentation by telling the students:

> *"I" Messages are a good way to communicate because an "I" Message cannot be changed or misunderstood. It is a direct and clear way to communicate. "I" Messages follow a format which we will spend some time discussing. Then you and a partner will role-play a conflict situation and use an "I" Message to resolve the conflict.*

Point to the "I" Message description written on the first piece of chart paper. Describe the format of an "I" Message. Then say:

> *I will give you an example of an "I" Message. Suppose your best friend sits with other people at lunch and ignores you. An "I" Message would be ...* (Point to the second message on the chart paper and read it aloud.)

> *It is possible to use the "I" Message format and not send an "I" Message, but a put-down.* (Point to the third message on the chart paper and read it aloud.)

> *Look at the difference between the two statements. The "I" Message lets the other person know how you are feeling without attacking or blaming him or her. There are no put-downs or name-calling in an "I" Message.*

Have the students look at the third message. Then ask:

> **Who can tell me which words in this statement make up a put-down?** (Circle the words the students name.)
>
> **How would you feel if someone said this to you?**
>
> **How would you react if someone said this to you?**
>
> **Would making this statement make the situation better or worse?**

The central goal of sending an "I" Message is to resolve the conflict. Reinforce this idea by saying:

> **Using a put-down will not resolve the conflict. It will only make the conflict worse. And using a put-down will almost guarantee that the conflict will continue. An "I" Message has the opposite effect of a put-down. That's because the focus of an "I" Message is on resolving the problem and not on getting even or hurting the other person.**

Activity Sheet: "I" Messages

Purpose: The purpose of this activity sheet is to have the students practice composing "I" Messages and recognize put-downs that are disguised as "I" Messages.

Materials Needed/Preparation: Make a copy of *"I" Messages* (page 69) for each student.

Distribute the activity sheet to each student. Then introduce the activity by saying:

> **There are two situations described on your activity sheet. We need to come up with "I" Messages that would work in each situation. In the first example, you catch your friend copying your homework assignment. Who can tell me what would be an appropriate "I" Message for this situation?** (Pause for responses.)
>
> **In the second situation, your friend is telling everyone one of your secrets. Who can tell me what would be an appropriate "I" Message for this situation?** (Pause for responses.)
>
> **Now that you have had practice with "I" Messages, I will assign each of you a partner. You and your partner will role-play each conflict and come up with your own "I" Message. When you have completed your role-play, write your "I" Messages on the activity sheet. Double check your "I" Messages to be sure they do not contain put-downs or blaming.**

Assign each student a partner. Then begin the activity.

Activity: Role-Playing Situation Cards

Purpose: The purpose of this activity is to familiarize students with the language and format of "I" Messages and how to use "I" Messages in different situations.

Materials Needed/Preparation: Make a copy of *Role-Play Practice: "I" Messages* (page 70) for each pair of students. Make a copy of the *Role-Playing Cards* (pages 71-72) and cut the cards apart. You may use the two blank cards to write additional situations.

Have the students remain with their partners. Distribute a *Role-Playing Card* and the activity sheet to each pair of students. Then say:

You will have five minutes to read your **Role-Playing Card**. *Write its number on your activity sheet. Then, working with your partner, you are to come up with two "I" Messages for your role-play and write them on your activity sheet. Decide which "I" Message you want to use and devise a role-play around it. When five minutes have elapsed, you and your partner will read the* **Role-Playing Card** *to the class and present your role-play, using the "I" Message of your choice.*

Have the students present their role-plays. When all of the role-plays and "I" Messages have been presented, ask:

Was this activity easy or difficult? Why?

Can you think of other situations in which you would use an "I" Message?

Lesson 5 Summary: "I" Messages

Conclude the lesson by saying:

This lesson looked at verbal communication and taught us that conflict can be resolved through effective communication. An "I" Message is a positive way to express feelings.

We looked at the format for "I" Messages. It is important to note that "I" Messages can be negative when they include put-downs. That is true even when the correct format is used.

You practiced writing and delivering your own "I" Messages in various situations.

Message Sending

NAME _____ DATE_____

Directions: Write down your observations of the groups as each one sends a message down the line.

GROUP #1 _____
_____

GROUP #2 _____
_____

GROUP #3 _____
_____

GROUP #4 _____
_____

What seemed to help the groups communicate the message accurately? _____

_____

_____

What seemed to interfere with communicating the message accurately? _____

_____

_____

"I" Messages

NAME _____ DATE_____

SITUATION 1: You catch a friend copying your homework.

I feel _____
(feeling)

when _____
(behavior)

because _____
(effects on you)

Example of negative "I" Message (put-down)

I feel like telling the whole school you cheated
(NOT A FEELING, BUT AN ACTION)

when you copied my homework
(BEHAVIOR)

because I want everyone to know you can't be trusted!
(NOT AN EFFECT ON YOU, BUT A DESIRE FOR REVENGE)

SITUATION 2: Your friend is telling everyone one of your secrets.

I feel _____
(feeling)

when _____
(behavior)

because _____
(effects on you)

Example of negative "I" Message (put down)

I feel like punching you
(NOT A FEELING, BUT AN ACTION)

when you blab stories about me all over
(BEHAVIOR WITH BLAME ATTACHED)

because you are such a liar.
(NOT AN EFFECT ON YOU, BUT NAME-CALLING)

HOW TO STOP BEFORE YOU POP © 2007 MAR✱CO PRODUCTS, INC. 1-800-448-2197

Role-Play Practice: "I" Messages

Partner #1 _____

Partner #2 _____

ROLE-PLAY CARD # [   ]

"I" MESSAGE #1

I feel _____
(write how you feel)

when _____
(stick to the facts and name the behavior)

because _____
(write how the behavior affects you)

"I" MESSAGE #2

I feel _____
(write how you feel)

when _____
(stick to the facts and name the behavior)

because _____
(write how the behavior affects you)

#1 Your friend says she won't be your friend any more if you play with someone else you like.

#2 Your friend sits with other kids at lunch and ignores you.

#3 Your friend is telling the whole school what boy or girl you think is cute.

#4 A student in your class gets mad when he loses in foursquare and throws temper tantrums.

#5 Your friend borrowed your videogame two weeks ago and hasn't given it back.

#6 A student in your class always begs for part of your lunch.

#7 A student in your class keeps teasing you about your new haircut.

#8 You have just heard that your best friend has been telling everyone that he/she doesn't really like you.

#9 A person at your table sings while you are trying to do your work.

#10 The person who sits next to you always sprawls across your desk area and crowds you.

#11 A classmate always asks you for paper, but never pays you back.

#12 Your friend tells you what kids you can and can't hang out with at recess.

#13 A classmate always rolls her eyes when you pass her in the hallway.

#14 A girl in your class is telling everyone that you have a crush on her.

#15 A classmate is telling everyone he beat you in basketball.

#16 A classmate is making fun of the brand of sneakers you are wearing.

#17 A boy in your class is telling everyone he can beat you in any sport.

#18 A classmate keeps making fun of your family.

#19

#20

LESSON 6
Putting It All Together

Materials Needed:

For the leader:
- ☐ Chalkboard and chalk or white board and marker
- ☐ List of things that make students angry (from Lesson 1)

For each student group:
- ☐ Copy of *Five Independent Tasks* (pages 81-83) *or Five Guided Tasks* (pages 84-86)
- ☐ Pencil

For each student:
- ☐ Copy of *Paper Popper Instructions* (page 87)
- ☐ Square piece of paper
- ☐ Blank piece of paper
- ☐ Pencil

Lesson:

(*Note*: Before presenting this lesson, decide whether the group will be presenting the *Five Guided Tasks* or the *Five Independent Tasks*. Make the decision based on the maturity and capabilities of the students in the group.)

Introduce the lesson by saying:

> **This is our last lesson. We are going to put to use all the things we have learned in all our lessons. I am going to divide you into groups. In your groups, you will work on five tasks. Each of the tasks will include things covered in our previous lessons.**

Write the following on the board:

The Five Tasks

1. Identify problem popper
2. List physical signs
3. Use calming strategies and get control of negative thoughts
4. Body Language
5. "I" Messages

Divide the students into groups.

Activity Sheet, Part 1: Identify The Problem Popper

Purpose: The purpose of this activity is for students to identify an area in their lives which tends to create tension and conflict.

Materials Needed/Preparation: Make a copy of *Five Independent Tasks* (pages 81-83) or *Five Guided Tasks* (pages 84-86) for each group of students.

Distribute the activity sheets and a pencil to each student group. Then introduce the activity by showing the students the list of things that made them angry from Lesson 1.

If you are using the *Five Independent Tasks* activity sheet, ask:

> *Remember when I listed the things that made you angry or ready to pop? In that lesson, we learned that most kids get really angry or pop when one of the things on that list occurs.*
>
> *Have your group pick one of the poppers from this list. On your activity sheet, write a real-life situation that includes that particular popper. Your group should write a scene that has happened or could happen to kids your age. Your scenes should be believable and based on experiences your group members have had or could have.*
>
> *Say your group picks copying as your popper. Your group could write a brief scene in which a student is copying from another student. The student could be copying classwork or copying another student's dress or behavior. In your scenes, do not use the names of real people. Why is it important not to use the names of real people in your scenes?* (Pause for responses.)

Give the students time to complete the task.

If you are using the *Five Guided Tasks* activity sheet, say:

> *Take a look at Page 1 of the* Five Guided Tasks *activity sheet. Eight common poppers are listed on that page. There is a scene that matches each popper. Read the choices and the scenes. Then, as a group, select one popper and check the box next to it.*

Give the students time to complete the task.

Activity Sheet, Part 2: Physical Signs

Purpose: The purpose of this activity is for students to identify and analyze their physical or physiological reactions to conflict.

Materials Needed/Preparation: None

If you are using the *Five Independent Tasks* activity sheet, discuss the physical signs that happen before you pop. Then say:

Continuing on Page 1 of your activity sheet, list the physical signs that are common among your group members. In other words, list which physical signs happen most often to the students in your group. For example, if most members of your group say that their hearts pound before they pop, list heart pounding on your activity sheet.

Give the students time to complete the task. Then say:

A lot of people have similar physical reactions when they get angry. Listening to others will teach you to pay more attention to what your body is saying before you feel overwhelmed by a tornado of emotions.

If you are using the *Five Guided Tasks* activity sheet, say:

Look at the list of physical signs on Page 2 of your activity sheets. Put a checkmark next to each physical sign each group member feels when he or she experiences a popper. On the blank line, add any signs that are not listed.

You will find that many of you have similar physical reactions when you become angry. Listening to the experiences of others will teach you to pay more attention to what your body is saying before you feel overwhelmed by a tornado of emotions.

Give the students time to complete the task.

Activity Sheet, Part 3: Calming Strategies And Controlling Your Thoughts

Purpose: The purpose of this activity is to help students learn to target specific activities, places, things, or people that help them achieve a sense of balance and calm.

Materials Needed/Preparation: None

If you are using the *Five Independent Tasks* activity sheet, say:

The Chinese Yin Yang symbolizes balance. When you are in danger of being swept up by a tornado of emotions or are about to pop, balance is important. Pick an activity, place, person, or thing that helps give most of your group members a sense of calm and balance. You may list more than one thing, because it is helpful to identify many different things or a variety of things that give you balance.

Give the students time to complete the task, then ask:

> *Who can tell me what I meant when I said, in an earlier lesson, that what you think is what you feel?* (When you think positive thoughts, you feel good; when you think negative thoughts, you feel bad.) *When you change your thoughts, you change your feelings. On your activity sheet, write the negative thoughts and feelings you associate with the popper you chose. Then change those negative thoughts and feelings to positive ones.*

Give the students time to complete the task.

If you are using the *Five Guided Tasks* activity sheet, say:

> *The Chinese Yin Yang symbolizes balance. When you are in danger of being swept up by a tornado of emotions or are about to pop, balance is important. As a group, identify and list different activities and people that help you find balance.*

Give the students time to complete the task.

Activity Sheet, Part 4: Body Language

Purpose: The purpose of this activity is for students to apply what they have learned about the importance of body language or nonverbal communication and how to best utilize these techniques when faced with a conflict.

Materials Needed/Preparation: None

If you are using the *Five Independent Tasks* activity sheet, say:

> *More than half of what we communicate is communicated through body language. On your activity sheet, list the body language that you will use to resolve the conflict. For example, you may write that you will use direct eye contact, keep your arms by your side, or another appropriate method.*

Give the students time to complete the task.

If you are using the *Five Guided Tasks* activity sheet, say:

> *It is important to identify appropriate nonverbal communication or body language. On your activity sheets, check all the body language or nonverbal behaviors that can improve communication and reduce conflict.*

Give the students time to complete the task.

Activity Sheet, Part 5: "I" Messages

Purpose: The purpose of this activity is for students to formulate an "I" Message using the given format and apply the "I" Message to a particular situation.

Materials Needed/Preparation: None

If you are using the *Five Independent Tasks* activity sheet, have the students use the "I' Message format to compose an "I" Message to use in the problem situation. (*Note*: Depending on their ages and interests, students may choose to role-play the information on the activity sheets or read the information, report-style, to the class. The leader may select one method for reporting the information or allow each group to decide how to report.)

If you are using the *Five Guided Tasks* activity sheet, have the students write a description of a situation and create an "I" Message using the given format. Remind the students to avoid put-downs.

Activity: Hole In Palm [7]

Purpose: The purpose of this activity is to demonstrate a simple optical illusion and relate it to resolving conflict.

Materials Needed/Preparation: Blank piece of paper and a pencil for each student.

Distribute a blank piece of paper and a pencil to each student. Then introduce the activity by saying:

> *You have all the tools you need to resolve any conflict that comes your way. We are going to perform an optical illusion experiment to test your abilities to see your way through conflict. On the blank sheet of paper, describe a conflict you are currently having. For example, you could write, "My brother hogs the computer and won't let me use it even though it is my turn."* (Pause until the students have done this.)

> *Roll the paper into a tube. Place the tube in front of one eye like a telescope and look at a distant object. Keep both eyes open.* (Pause until the students have done this.)

---

7. Taken from: www.partymagic.50megs.com/custom2.html.

HOW TO STOP BEFORE YOU POP © 2007 MAR✳CO PRODUCTS, INC. 1-800-448-2197

Bend your other arm so that your palm is facing you. Bring the palm of your free hand up next to the paper tube. What do you notice in the palm of your hand? (Pause for responses.)

Yes, you see a hole. How does this optical illusion relate to our lessons on conflict and anger management? (Pause for responses.) *Conflict may stop you sometimes. An upward palm is a gesture that means, "Stop." When you use the techniques you learned in these lessons, you can see your way through the conflict. The skills you have learned will enable you to create an opening that leads to a resolution.*

Activity: Paper Popper Pattern [8]

Purpose: The purpose of this activity is for students to create a take-home visual reminder of the lessons on dealing with conflict.

Materials Needed/Preparation: Make a copy of the *Paper Popper Instructions* (page 87) for each student. You also need a square piece of paper for each student.

Distribute the instructions and a square piece of paper to each student. Then introduce the activity by saying:

We have learned to control our feelings by controlling our thoughts. You know that you have power over what you are thinking and what you are feeling. You can control when you pop.

Using your square piece of paper and Paper Popper Instructions, you are going to make a paper popper you can take home.

Have each student follow the directions and make a paper popper. Then say:

The paper popper is something you can control, just like you can control your own poppers. Raise your arm. Quickly swing your arm down and listen for the pop. Just as you control your paper popper, you also control your anger.

Lesson 6 Summary: Putting It All Together

Conclude the unit by saying:

In this lesson, we reviewed everything we learned in previous lessons. We learned five tasks that can help us resolve conflicts.

---

8. Taken from: McGill, Ormond (1992) *Paper Magic: Creating Fantasies and Performing Tricks With Paper.* Brookfield, CT: The Millbrook Press, 1992.

1. *Identify the problem*
2. *Identify physical signs*
3. *Calming strategies*
4. *Body language*
5. *"I" Messages*

We also learned how to apply each of the five tasks. In our final lesson, we performed an optical illusion in which we "saw" a hole in our palm. The hole represents an opening or passage. The five tasks are skills that provide an opening or passage through conflict and anger.

Then we made paper poppers. Always remember that you control the popper. The popper does not control you.

In summary, we have learned many methods to help us manage anger. We:

- *looked at all the interactions encountered through contact with different groups*

- *discussed the two main reasons for conflict—possessions/resources and values/needs*

- *saw that conflict can occur between individuals, groups, or even countries*

- *learned that both conflict and anger can be used in productive and positive ways that can actually improve relationships*

- *analyzed what happens inside our bodies when we get angry*

- *talked about things that help us gain balance and restore calm when we are faced with conflict*

- *practiced visualization exercises with a* Power Test

- *learned that what we think is what we feel and that when we control our thoughts, we control our feelings*

- *became familiar with the importance of nonverbal communication or body language and the role nonverbal techniques play in communication*

- *practiced creating "I" Messages and combining them with appropriate gestures to improve communication*

- *ended with an activity in which we reviewed the five steps needed to manage anger and resolve conflict:*

    1. *Identify the problem*
    2. *Identify physical signs*
    3. *Use calming strategies*
    4. *Correctly use and interpret body language*
    5. *`Use "I" Messages*

Now you have everything you need to stop before you pop!

Five Independent Tasks

Names _____

1. **Identify The Problem Popper**

Directions: Group members pick a common popper.

Example: Our popper is cheating in games.

Our popper is: _____

_____

Directions: Write a short scene in which the popper appears.

Example: Two kids are playing a board game. One kid rolls the dice and the dice falls on the floor. The kid who rolled the dice claims that the number on the dice was a 6. The other kid claims he/she saw the number 4 on the dice.

Scene in which the popper appears: _____

_____

_____

_____

_____

2. **Physical Signs**

Directions: Group members list physical signs they commonly experience when faced with a popper.

Example: Our physical signs of poppers are heart pounding, flushed face, grinding teeth, and headache.

Our physical signs of poppers are: _____

_____

_____

3. Calming Strategies and Controlling Your Thoughts

CALMING STRATEGIES

Directions: Group members list activities, things, people, or places that give them a sense of calm or balance.

Example: The things that help us find balance and calm us down are sports, spending time with our pets, listening to music, and talking with our friends.

The things that help us find balance and calm us down are: _____

_____

_____

_____

_____

_____

CONTROLLING THOUGHTS

Directions: Group members list all the negative thoughts and feelings its chosen popper causes.

Example: Negative thoughts: I can't stand playing games with him/her. What a cheater! This is so unfair. I should throw the dice in his/her face.

Negative feelings = annoyance and frustration

Example: Positive thoughts: I know he/she is cheating, but it is only a game. I will tell him/her that if he/she doesn't play fair, I will not continue to play this game.

Positive feelings = accomplishment and relief

Negative thoughts and feelings associated with the popper are: _____

_____

_____

_____

_____

Positive thoughts and feelings associated with the popper: _____

_____

_____

_____

_____

4. Body Language

Directions: Group members list the nonverbal gestures or body language they will use when communicating about the popper.

Example: Our group will communicate nonverbally by using direct eye contact, keeping our hands by our sides, and standing still.

Our group will communicate nonverbally by: _____

_____

_____

_____

_____

5. "I" Message

Directions: Group members compose an "I" Message to communicate about the popper.

Example: When you say that your dice had a number I didn't see, I feel frustrated because I can't trust that you are playing this game fairly.

The "I" Message for our group is: _____

_____

_____

_____

Five Guided Tasks

Names _____

1.   Identify The Problem Popper

Directions: Group members pick a common popper from the list below.

☐ Cheating   ☐ Copying Work
☐ Lying   ☐ Copying Style
☐ Stealing   ☐ Messing With Your Stuff
☐ Name-Calling/Teasing   ☐ Talking Behind Your Back

Directions: Group members pick a scene below that matches their common popper.

Cheating: During a card game, one kid tried to hide the extra cards drawn so he/she would win. The other kids tell him/her to stand up, because they suspect he/she is sitting on the extra cards.

Lying: A student says that he/she is flying in a private jet to Las Vegas over Winter Break. The other students don't believe it and ask him/her to prove it.

Stealing: A group of students is sitting at a table. A pink eraser belonging to a student at the next table has fallen to the floor. A student at the first table grabs the eraser and quickly writes his/her name on it. The student who dropped the eraser notices that it is missing and sees what looks like his/her missing eraser at the next table. The student who picked up the eraser refuses to give it back. He/she claims that he/she found the eraser, which has his/her name on it.

Name-Calling/Teasing: A student continually gets picked on because of his/her last name.

Copying Work: A student sitting at a table with a group of students doesn't complete his/her assignments and tries to get the answers from other kids at the table.

Copying Style: A student starts copying a popular student's expressions and mannerisms in order to be more like him/her.

Messing With Your Stuff: A younger brother/sister keeps coming into your room and messing with your stuff. You keep asking him/her to stop, but he/she laughs at you.

Talking Behind Your Back: A group of kids has told you that a certain friend talks behind your back. When you confront the friend, he/she denies it and says the other kids are lying.

2. Physical Signs

Directions: Group members should place a checkmark next to each of the physical signs they experience when they experience a popper.

☐ Heart Pounding   ☐ Teeth Grinding
☐ Clenched/Tight Muscles   ☐ Sweating
☐ Flushed Face   ☐ Crying
☐ Headache   ☐ Shaking/Trembling
☐ Ears Ringing   ☐ Other _____

3. Calming Strategies and Controlling Your Thoughts

Directions: For the categories below, group members list items that help them find balance and calm down when faced with a popper.

Activities _____

People _____

Places_____

Events _____

Things_____

Directions: From the choices below, group members pick a thought and feeling that will help them solve the problem.

Thought = No big deal! I don't like this, but I can deal with it!
Feeling = Focused

Thought = How can I stop this from happening? I need a plan.
Feeling = Calm

Thought = I need to show that I can handle this even though I am annoyed.
Feeling = Level-headed

Thought = I don't really think I am being treated fairly. How can I change this?
Feeling = Assertive

4. Body Language

Directions: From the list below, group members check all the body language or nonverbal behaviors that can improve communication and reduce conflict.

- ☐ Eye contact
- ☐ Arms by sides
- ☐ Nodding
- ☐ Standing
- ☐ Hands on hips
- ☐ Straight face
- ☐ Sitting
- ☐ Arms folded
- ☐ Smiling

☐ Others _____

5. "I" Message:

Directions: Using the format below, group members are to create an "I" Message that fits their selected situation. Fill in the blanks with words. Be careful to avoid put-downs.

Write your common popper situation again here: _____

_____

_____

_____

"I" Message format:

I feel _____

(fill in a feeling word)

when _____

(fill in the behavior)

because _____

(fill in the effects the behavior has on you)

"I" Message situation example:

I feel frustrated
when you tell everyone you are only pretending to be my friend
because I feel like I can't really trust you.

Paper Popper Instructions

You need a square piece of paper of any size.

Fold the paper in half to form a triangle.

Open the paper and fold it the other way.

Open the folded paper and you will see an *X*.

Fold the paper in half. On the front of the folded paper, you will see an imprint of one of the triangles.

Push in the sides of the paper into the center to form a triangle.

Place your index finger between the folds and swing your hand down quickly.

HOW TO STOP BEFORE YOU POP © 2007 MAR*CO PRODUCTS, INC. 1-800-448-2197

Kathie Guild

Kathie Guild is an elementary school counselor in Chapel Hill, North Carolina. She lives with her husband and daughter and a variety of pets.

Other Books by Kathie Guild

Froggy and Friends I
Froggy and Friends II
More Froggy and Friends
Everyone Is Included